English for Standardized Tests

by

SGK Teaches

To Aryan and Sahana

About the Author

Srinivasa Sastri Siravuri offers very unique and innovative ways of teaching for standardized tests. Siravuri's academic qualifications include a Ph.D. in engineering. Siravuri has many years of experience coaching students for standardized tests. Throughout this book, Siravuri offers many time saving tips, short cuts and tricks to help students do well with standardized tests.

Website: www.sgkteaches.com

E-mail: sgk@sgkteaches.com

ISBN-13: 978-0692893456

ISBN-10: 0692893458

Library of Congress Control Number: 2017909564

Contents

1. Introduction

Standardized tests are not easy to crack. Knowing the concepts will not ensure success in the standardized tests. *Applying* the concepts is even more important than *knowing the concepts*. Sometimes a problem involves applying multiple concepts as illustrated in this book.

Although English grammar is an important aspect of the test, there are other aspects of the test that are equally important:

- Pattern Recognition
  - There are only a limited number of question patterns. Familiarizing yourself with the question patterns goes a long way in improving your score.
- Time Management
  - Always read the answer choices first. Answer choices give you important clues about the question pattern. It will come with practice. If you recognize the pattern, you increase your chances of answering the question accurately and quickly.
- Analytical Thinking
  - There is **only one correct** answer for any given question.
  - This fact can be used effectively in the process of elimination.

Review the following problems to understand what this book is about.

Example: There is a quick fix to the problem. <u>However</u>, Mary looked for a long term solution.

    A. NO CHANGE.   B. Consequently,

    C. As a result,   D. Hence,

I notice a student reading the question and answer choices several times before picking his or her answer. As a result, the student is losing valuable time, a resource that shall be managed wisely. Instead, one can arrive at the answer more quickly by employing techniques outlined in this book.

Are you able to recognize the pattern by glancing at the answer choices? The concept being tested is "Transitional Phrases."

Once you recognize the pattern, note that three of the choices, choice B, choice C and choice D have a similar meaning. **Because there cannot be more than one correct answer choice**, one can eliminate all three choices B, C and D. Choice A stands out from the rest.

Final check – once you narrowed the answer to Choice A, plug it into the sentence to validate whether the sentence makes sense or not. Underline *quick fix* and *long term solution*. The sentence is looking for a contrast. Hence, choice A works.

Example: John is an <u>eloquent speaker</u>.

    A. NO CHANGE.   B. eloquently speaking.

    C. eloquently speaker.   D. eloquent speaking.

Are you able to recognize the pattern by glancing at the answer choices? The pattern is "Adjectives and Adverbs." Typically, for this type of a question, two choices (choices A and D) mention an adjective and two choices (choices B and C) mention an adverb.

Once you recognize the pattern, note that adverbs modify *verbs, adverbs or adjectives* whereas adjectives modify *nouns or pronouns*. Because *speaker* is a noun, a word modifying it should be an adjective. *Eloquent* is an adjective and *eloquently* is an adverb. Hence, one can eliminate choices B and C. Choice D combines an adjective with a verb and hence, can be eliminated. Choice A combines an adjective with a noun and hence, it is grammatically correct. The best answer is choice A.

Example: A reality show signed up a large number of volunteers, many <u>of which</u> are not aware of what's in store.

    A. NO CHANGE.   B. of who
    C. of whom   D. of whose

Are you able to recognize the pattern by glancing at the answer choices? The concept being tested is *Who vs. Whom & Whoever vs. Whomever*. Typically, for this type of a question, one choice includes *who* and a second choice includes *whom*.

Once you recognize the pattern, note that *who* is used to refer to the subjects and *whom* is used to refer to the objects. *Of* is a preposition. Prepositional phrases are followed by objects. Volunteers is the object, hence *whom* is correct. For example, it is all right to say *many of them* or *many of us*. It is incorrect to say *many of they* or *many of we*.

Hence, choice C is the best answer.

Example: By examining the results from a series of experiments, <u>a new discovery was able to be found by the scientists</u>.

    A. NO CHANGE.   B. a new discovery was made possible.
    C. the scientists made a new discovery.   D. a new discovery was made possible by scientists.

Are you able to recognize the pattern by glancing at the answer choices? The concept being tested is *Adjective Phrase or Participle Phrase*. Adjectives modify nouns and pronouns. Similarly, adjective phrases also modify nouns or pronouns. In the example, *By examining the results from a series of experiments* is an adjective phrase. Hence, it is modifying a noun. An adjective phrase must be immediately followed by the noun it modifies. In this instance, it is the scientists who are examining the results, not the discovery. Hence, the adjective phrase should be followed by the scientists. Choice C is the best answer.

Example: The United States launched a major campaign to deter terrorism. The outcome of the campaign <u>yet still remains to be seen</u>.

    A. NO CHANGE.   B. yet still to be unknown mystery.
    C. yet remains to be seen.   D. remains unknown.

Are you able to recognize the pattern by glancing at the answer choices? The concept being tested is "Redundancy or Wordiness." The test does not like redundancy or wordiness. Instead, the test likes simple or concise answer choices. *Yet* and *Still remains to be seen* mean the same. *Unknown* and *mystery* also mean the same. Hence, choices A, B and C can be eliminated. Choice D is the best answer.

2. Building Blocks

In this chapter, we will review the most common question patterns in the English portion of the test. Let me ask you a few questions first. Do you happen to play sports? What does it take to win a game?

Winning a game involves four main strategies.

1. Knowing the rules on how to play the game.
2. A lot of practice.
3. Knowing your opponent and outsmarting your opponent.
4. Executing your strategies and not falling for the traps set by the opponent.

The strategies as demonstrated and applied in this book help students improve their score in a standardized test.

Before I show you how the game is played, I need to introduce you to the game jargon.

Building Blocks of English Grammar

Noun: Nouns refer to a person, place or thing. One function of a noun is to act as a subject of a sentence.

Example: **John** will be taking the test next month. *John* is the subject of the sentence.

Although there is a lot to learn about nouns, three items that come in handy in the test are listed below.

1. Noun + Reflexive Pronoun: A noun and reflexive pronoun are treated as one unit and hence, do not require any punctuation in between the two. A detailed explanation is given when we discuss pattern 9 later in this chapter.

Example:

Wrong: **Myself** went to the market. Reflexive pronoun cannot stand by itself.

Wrong: **I, myself** went to the market. Do not separate subject and reflexive pronoun with a comma.

Correct: **I myself** went to the market.

2. Title + Proper Noun: A title and proper noun are treated as one unit and hence, they do not require any punctuation in between the two. A detailed explanation is given when we discuss pattern 6 later in this chapter.

Example: *President Trump' Vice President Pence*

Wrong: Well known for his research, **nuclear scientist, Smith** made an interesting discovery. This sentence is grammatically correct. However, the test prefers to treat a title and proper noun as one unit.

Correct: Well known for his research, **nuclear scientist Smith** made an interesting discovery.

3. Gerund, a verb acting as a noun: Sometimes, a verb can act as a noun.

Example: **Walking** is a good exercise. *Walking* is acting as a noun and a subject.

Example: **Shopping** is fun. *Shopping* is acting as a noun and a subject.

Verb: There are two types of verbs: verbs indicating action and verbs indicating a state of being.

Examples of verbs indicating action are talking, walking, speaking and jumping etc. Examples of verbs indicating a state of being are is, am, and was etc.

Example: John is **swimming**. *Swimming* is an action verb.

Example: I **am** hungry. *Am* is a verb indicating a state of being.

Pronoun: Pronoun refers to a noun. Three golden rules of pronoun usage are listed below.

Rule 1: Pronoun should match the subject in gender and in number (i.e. singular or plural).

Example:

Wrong: The public library implemented many changes to meet the needs of **their** patrons. Library is singular. Hence, the pronoun **their** is an incorrect reference.

Correct: The public library implemented many changes to meet the needs of **its** patrons.

Indefinite pronouns listed below are considered singular.

Every**one**, No**one**, Some**one** and **None**. Note that "**one**" means only one, not many.

Every**body**, No**body**, Some**body**. Similarly, "**body**" means one body, not many bodies.

Example:

Wrong: Some**body** left **their** car lights on.

Correct: Some**body** left **his or her** car lights on.

Example:

Wrong: No**one** submitted **their** proposal yet.

Correct: Noone submitted **his or her** proposal yet.

Example:

Wrong: The coach asked every**body** to bring **their** uniforms.

7

Correct: The coach asked every**body** to bring **his or her** uniform.

Rule 2: Pronoun reference should be clear.

Example:

Wrong: John told his father that **he** needs to see a doctor. In the sentence, it is not clear whether **he** refers to John or his father. Who needs to see a doctor, John or his father?

Correct: John told his father that **John** needs to see a doctor. (OR) John told his father that **his father** needs to see a doctor.

Rule 3: Distinguish between subject and object pronouns.

Subject Pronouns	Object Pronouns
I	Me
We	Us
You	You
He	Him
She	Her
They	Them
Who	Whom
Whoever	Whomever

Use a subject pronoun when a sentence needs a subject and use an object pronoun when a sentence needs an object. Always remember *a preposition* needs an *object*.

Example:

Wrong: Between she and I, there are no secrets. *Between* is a preposition and hence, it needs an object pronoun.

Correct: Between her and me, there are no secrets.

Example:

Wrong: I ordered a latte for you and I. *For* is a preposition and hence, it needs an object pronoun.

Correct: I ordered a latte for you and me.

Adjectives and Adverbs: Adjectives qualify a noun or a pronoun. Adverbs qualify a verb, adverb or adjective.

Example: He is a **kind** man. **Kind** is acting as an adjective. It qualifies man. What kind of a man is he? He is a **kind** man.

Example: He acted **kindly**. **Kindly** is acting as an adverb. It qualifies how the man acted. How did the man act? He acted **kindly**.

Prepositions: Prepositions connect **objects** to a sentence. Examples of prepositions include **in, out, inside, outside, between, with, for, to, under, underneath, over, off**, and **of**. A preposition cannot stand by itself. A preposition needs an object.

Prepositional Phrase	Object
Inside the house	**house** is the object.
On the table	**table** is the object.
In the car	**car** is the object.
With You and me	**You and me** are the objects.
Between You and her	**You and her** are the objects.
For them	**Them** is the object.

As noted earlier, prepositions are followed by objects. Hence, the following pronoun references are incorrect.

Example:

Wrong: With you and **I**, between you and **she** and for **they**.

Correct: With you and **me**, between you and **her** and for **them**.

Conjunction: A **conjunction** connects two sentences or a sentence and a phrase. There are two types of conjunctions: **coordinated and subordinate**.

A coordinated conjunction connects two sentences that are of equal importance (also referred to as equal rank). "**And**," "**or**," "**either..or**," "**neither..nor**" and "**so**" are coordinated conjunctions.

Example: We went to market **and** bought presents.

Example: Either John **or** Mary should be in the office.

A subordinate conjunction connects a sentence and a phrase. "**While**," "**because**" and "**although**" are subordinate conjunctions.

Example: **Because** it was raining, we did not go out.

"Because it was raining" is not a full sentence. It is a sentence fragment. "We did not go out" is a full sentence. Typically, a subordinate conjunction connects a sentence fragment to a full sentence. A sentence fragment and a complete sentence are separated by a comma, not a period.

Example: **While** I waited for John, I finished my homework.

"While I waited for John" is a sentence fragment. "I finished my homework" is a full sentence.

Sentence Structure

A typical sentence has a subject. Subject is the one performing action or subject is what the sentence is talking about. Subject and corresponding verb should be consistent in a sentence. Similarly, subject and pronoun should be consistent in a sentence. Finally, the tense (present, past and future tense) should be consistent in a sentence.

Independent and Dependent Sentences

An independent clause or sentence is one that can stand by itself. "I finished my homework" is an independent sentence. An independent sentence is followed by a period or a semicolon. "While I waited for John" is a dependent clause because it cannot stand by itself. The clause needs an independent sentence. A dependent clause is typically separated from the independent clause with a comma.

Run-on Sentence

A run-on sentence is one with no proper punctuation.

Example:

Wrong: After you complete your homework you can play. The sentence is missing a comma.

Correct: After you complete your homework, you can play.

Example:

Wrong: We went to the market purchased fruits and vegetables. The sentence is missing a conjunction.

Correct: We went to the market and purchased fruits and vegetables.

Punctuation

It is helpful to understand how the following punctuation elements work.

Period and Semicolon

A period and a semicolon work the same way. They are both interchangeable. A period and a semicolon separate two full sentences (two independent sentences). It is incorrect to separate a dependent clause (or sentence fragment) and an independent clause/sentence with a period or a semicolon.

Example:

Wrong: While I waited for John; I finished my homework.

Correct: While I waited for John, I finished my homework.

Comma

A comma introduces a pause in a sentence. A comma separates a dependent clause and an independent clause. It is incorrect to separate two independent sentences with a comma.

Example:

Wrong: We went to the mall, purchased presents.

Correct: We went to the mall and purchased presents. (OR) We went to the mall; we purchased presents.

Two Commas or two dashes or two parentheses

Two commas or two dashes typically introduce non-essential information. If we remove what is between the two commas or two dashes, the sentence should still be grammatically correct.

Example:

The President, along with his cabinet, arrived at the White House.

Example:

I met Mrs. Liz – my daughter's music teacher – at the concert.

Colon

A colon introduces a list. Most importantly, what comes before a colon should be an independent sentence. A colon cannot separate two independent sentences.

In addition, a colon can be used to introduce *a list with only one item*. For some reason, the test likes to test usage of a colon when introducing a list with only one item. The following sentence is perfectly fine.

Example:

Correct: We were focused on only one thing: getting out of the hole in which we put ourselves.

Example:

Wrong: We shopped for: a jacket, a tie and a belt. "We shopped for" is *not* an independent sentence and hence, it cannot be followed by a colon.

Correct: We shopped for three things: a jacket, a tie and a belt. "We shopped for three things" is an independent sentence (not a fragment) and hence, it can be followed by a colon.

<u>A Single Dash</u>

A single dash introduces a definition.

<u>Example</u>:

The jury reached a verdict – guilty.

<u>Example</u>:

The house rule is simple – clean up after yourself.

3. Question Patterns

Now that you understand the basics of English grammar, it is time to get yourself familiar with the most common question patterns from the standardized tests.

1. Transitional Phrases

There are several types of transitional phrases. The two common types are ones that introduce a contrast and the ones that reinforce.

To introduce contrast	Reinforcing	Comparison	Adding More	Give Examples
Yet	Consequently	By the same token	Besides	For example
Even (though)	Hence	Likewise	Further	For instance
Nethertheless	Therefore	In the same way	Also	
Nonetheless	Thus	In the same manner	In addition	
But	Because	Similarly	Moreover	
To the contrary	As a result of		Furthermore	
On the other hand	Hence			
As opposed to	Accordingly			
However				
Although or though				
Contrastingly				
In contrast				
While				
Notwithstanding				

For questions involving transitional phrases, always read the previous sentence. Eliminate choices that have the same meaning or ones that introduce the same type of transition.

2. Redundancy/Wordiness

The following table lists several examples of redundant phrases.

Examples of Redundant Phrases
Yet even
Each and everyone
The reason why or the reason because
Same/Exact identical
Unexpected surprise
Past history
Very unique or most unique
Since the time when
Final end
Ascend up or descend down
Revert back
Repeat again

Postpone till later
End result
Difficult dilemma
Close proximity
At the present time
Advance warning/fore warning
New innovations

Simple is better. Eliminate choices that have redundant phrases and choices that are wordy.

3. Subject Verb Agreement

Both subject and verb in a sentence should be consistent. Singular subjects take singular verbs and plural (more than one) subjects take plural verbs.

Example: She goes to church every Sunday. "She" is a singular subject and "goes" is a singular verb.

We go to church every Sunday. "We" is a plural subject and "go" is a plural verb.

a. Subject and verb separated by irrelevant information

One of the most common traps in the test is subject and verb agreement. Surprisingly, most students fall for this trap. When a subject includes a qualifier with additional details, the qualifier is irrelevant when picking the appropriate verb.

Example:

Wrong: The mountain *with its spectacular colors* attract tourists every year.

Correct: The mountain with its spectacular colors attracts tourists every year.

"Mountain" is a singular subject. "Attracts" is a singular verb.

The elements of this type of a question include the following:

- The subject and verb are intentionally separated by irrelevant information.
- The noun (spectacular colors) before the verb is made to be plural to trick the students.

To simplify the sentence, remove the irrelevant information "with its spectacular colors" and read the sentence as "The mountain attracts tourists every year."

Example:

Wrong: The funding *for the inner-city school districts* were cut again this year.

Correct: The funding *for the inner-city school districts* was cut again this year.

The subject is "funding" and the verb is "was cut." Read the sentence as "The funding was cut again this year."

Example:

Wrong: The <u>statue</u> with its many faces and hands <u>awe</u> the viewers.

Correct: The <u>statue</u> with its many faces and hands <u>awes</u> the viewers.

The author recommends two techniques to tackle questions involving this concept.

1. **Remove the qualifier/irrelevant information and read the sentence. Using this technique, the following sentences are simplified as illustrated.**

   The mountain ~~with its spectacular views~~ attracts tourists every year.
   The funding ~~for the inner-city schools~~ was cut again this year.
   The statue ~~with its many faces and hands~~ awes the viewers.

2. **Form a question for which the sentence becomes the answer.**

   What attracts tourists every year? <u>Mountain,</u> which is the subject of the sentence.
   What was cut again this year? <u>Funding</u>.
   What awes the viewers? <u>Statue</u>.

b. **Compound Subjects**

Compound subjects are multiple subjects combined by one of the following: and, or, either … or, and neither … nor.

<u>And</u>: And almost always indicates a plural subject. It means more than one.

Example: <u>Jack and Mary</u> are in the race.

Jack and Mary are two subjects and hence, they make a plural subject.

Example: <u>The precise magnitude and the location</u> of the earthquake are yet to be identified.

Magnitude and location are two subjects and hence, they make a plural subject.

<u>Or</u>: Subjects combined with "or" are tricky. Make sure you match the verb with the closest subject. Simplify the sentence by removing "or" and everything before it.

Example: Mary or <u>her parents</u> are going to guide us with the tour.

Parents is the closest subject and hence, the correct verb is "are."   Simplify the sentence as indicated below:

~~Mary or~~ her parents are going to guide us with the tour.

Her parents or Mary is going to guide us with the tour.

Mary is the closest subject and hence, the correct verb is "is." Simplify the sentence as indicated below:

~~Her parents or~~ Mary is going to guide us with the tour.

Either … Or and Neither … Nor: Subjects combined with "either … or " and "neither … nor" work the same way as subjects combined with "or."   Make sure you match the verb with the closest subject. Simplify the sentence by removing everything before the second subject.

Example: Either Mary or her parents are going to guide us with the tour.   Simplify the sentence as indicated below:

~~Either Mary or~~ her parents are going to guide us with the tour.

Neither Mary nor her parents are going to help us. Simplify the sentence as indicated below:

~~Neither Mary nor~~ her parents are going to help us.

Do not mix up "either .. or" and "neither … nor" The following sentences are incorrect.

Neither Mary or her parents are going to help us. "Or" should be changed to "nor."

Either Mary nor her parents are going to help us. "Nor" should be changed to "or."

4. Subject Pronoun Agreement

Refer to the pronoun and prepositions discussed in the previous chapter. Refer to the rules of a pronoun (p.7).

5. Who vs Whom & Whoever vs. Whomever

Use who and whoever when a sentence needs a subject and use whom and whomever when a sentence needs an object.

Example: My parents, who are in India, informed me about my sister's well-being.

Parents is the subject. Hence, *who* is the appropriate pronoun to use.

Example: Whom did you give the phone to? Whom did you speak to? Whom did you mean?

I gave the phone to *him/her*. I spoke to *him/her*. I meant *him/her.* Questions involving *whom* result in an answer involving *him/her*.

Example: Each year, the United States attracts immigrants, many of *whom* contribute greatly to the economy.

<u>Example</u>: Though it is cold, the game attracted many spectators, all of *whom* were wearing warm clothes.

Of is a preposition and hence, is followed by *whom*, not *who*.

6. Punctuation

Refer to the previous chapter to learn the concepts related to a comma, semicolon, period, colon, single dash and two dashes.

7. Title and Subject

A title followed by a subject (a proper name) needs no commas. The title and the proper name together form the subject of the sentence.

<u>Example</u>:

<u>Wrong</u>: Astro-physicist, James Stewart, proposed a new theory to explain the dark matter.

<u>Correct</u>: Astro-physicist James Stewart proposed a new theory to explain the dark matter.

Standardized tests do not like adding a comma between the name and the title. "Astro-physicist" is not specific enough. Although "James Stewart" is a proper name, the individual writing this sentence might want to emphasize "Astro-physicist James Stewart." Commas after the title are appropriate only when the reference is clear to the reader. In the example, adding the commas is all right if the reader knows the writer of the sentence means "James Stewart." Given there are many Astro-physicists, it is better to omit the commas so that it is clear the writer is referring to "Astro-physicist James Stewart," not any astro-physicist and not any James Stewart.

8. Exceptions of Possessive Case

Possessive case indicates ownership. Typically, a possessive case is formed by adding an apostrophe and "s" after a noun. Several examples of simple possessive case are listed below.

John's house, earth's atmosphere, moon's gravitational force, country's diversity, Mary's desk.

There are two exceptions to the possessive case.

1. Its and It's

Often, students get confused between the two. "Its" is a possessive form of "it." For example, "its color" means the color of something one is referring to. "Its surface" means the surface of something one is referring to.

On the other hand, it's is a contraction of "it is." There is no possessive case implied here. For example, "it's raining" means "it is raining." "It's simple" means "it is simple."

2. Nouns ending in s

Nouns ending in s take apostrophe. But apostrophe is not followed by an *s*.

Examples: Jones' house, James' car, horses' stable (and not Jones's house, James's car, horses's stable).

9. Reflexive Pronoun

Reflexive pronouns are used to place extra emphasis.

Example:

I myself wrote this journal. "I myself" together is the subject and do not separate "I" and "myself" with a comma.

Example:

She herself cleaned the floor. "She herself" is the subject and do not separate "She" and "herself" with a comma.

The following two forms are incorrect because "herself cleaned the floor" does not make sense.

She, herself, cleaned the floor.

She, herself cleaned the floor.

There is no shadow without an object. One cannot see anything in a mirror unless an object is in front of the mirror. Similarly, reflexive pronouns cannot be used as a subject on their own.

In this question type always pick a choice where the reflexive pronoun is **not separated by commas** from the main subject.

10. Use of Two Commas or Two Dashes or Two Parentheses

Two commas or two dashes introduce non-essential information. Hence, information within two commas or two dashes can be removed to simplify the sentence.

Example:

We, however, remained in touch with each other. The sentence can be simplified as "We remained in touch with each other."

Example:

The statue, with many faces and hands, looked scary. The statue looked scary.

11. Adjectives and Adverbs

Adjectives modify nouns or pronouns. Adverbs modify verbs, adverbs or adjectives.

Examples of Adjective	Examples of Adverb
He is a **kind** man	He acted **kindly**.
It is an **elegant** solution.	She walked **elegantly**.
We bought a **soft** toy.	He spoke **softly**.
We walked at a **brisk** pace.	We walked **briskly**.
He is a **bright** student.	The stadium is **brightly** lit.

Typically, one can tell the concept being tested is adjective and adverb because two of the four choices are listed with an adjective and the two other choices are listed with an adverb.

Example: The mathematician laid out an <u>elegantly solution</u> to the theorem.

    A. NO CHANGE.   B. elegant solution

    C. elegantly looking   D. elegant solutions

What is being modified is "solution." What type of a solution is it? It is an elegant solution. "Solution" is a noun and hence, it needs an adjective. Choice D is incorrect because "an elegant solutions" is wrong. "Elegant" is an adjective. Choice B is correct.

12. Adjective Phrase or Participle Phrase

An adjective phrase modifies the noun that comes immediately after the phrase. Make sure an adjective phrase is modifying the right subject (the subject it intends to modify).

Example:

<u>Wrong</u>: Stranded at the airport, the bags were delayed.

<u>Correct</u>: Stranded at the airport, we found our bags delayed.

Who is or what is stranded at the airport? We are stranded at the airport, not the bags.

Example:

<u>Wrong</u>: Walking into the parking lot, the vehicle lights were flashing.

<u>Correct</u>: Walking into the parking lot, I found the vehicle lights were flashing.

Ask yourself, who is or what is walking into the parking lot? I walked into the parking lot, not the vehicle lights.

Example:

Wrong: Studying hard for the test, the score was improved.

Correct: Studying hard for the test, I improved my score.

Who is or what is studying for the test? I studied hard for the test, not the score.

13. Parallel Structure

It is recommended to maintain parallel structure within a sentence. Note the examples as listed below.

Example:

Wrong: I enjoy hiking, playing tennis and to read books.

Correct: I enjoy hiking, playing tennis and reading books. "Reading" should be parallel to "hiking" and "playing."

Students find it challenging when "parallel structure" is combined with "not only...but also".

If "not only" is followed by a noun, then "but also" should be followed by a noun.

Example:

Wrong: I enjoy not only hiking but also to read books.

Correct: I enjoy not only hiking but also reading books. (OR) I enjoy not only to hike but also to read books.

14. Faulty Comparison or Illogical Comparison

When comparing two things, one needs to ensure that the items being compared are like things.

Example:

Wrong: The population of India is greater than the United States.

Correct: The population of India is greater than the population of the United States.

Note the population of India cannot be compared to the United States. Instead, the population of India should be compared to the population of the United States.

Example:

Wrong: A cobra's bite is more dangerous than a scorpion.

Correct: A cobra's bite is more dangerous than a scorpion's bite.

Note that <u>a cobra's bite</u> cannot be compared to a scorpion. Instead, <u>a cobra's bite</u> should be compared to <u>a scorpion's bite</u>.

15. Verb Tense

Verb tense relates to present tense, past tense and future tense. Typically, a question related to verb tense can be answered by looking for clues in the narration. Try to keep the verb tense consistent with the rest of the narration.

16. YES- or NO-type Questions

When a question has two answers that start with YES and two answers with NO, it is advantageous for you to first decide whether you are going to answer the question as YES or NO. Once you decide, focus only on two choices that are relevant. Recognize that you do not need to read all four choices. It will save you valuable time on the test when you are not reading the choices that you do not need to read. Although the time saved appears to be insignificant, if there are several questions on the test that are of this type, you are likely to save several minutes and hence, overall, it will help you manage your time better.

17. Underline Questions

For certain questions, it helps to underline key phrases or words in the question to bring attention to the relevant information.

<u>Example</u>: Noting that all choices are true, what best illustrates ..

Underline illustrates. Illustrates means examples. Look for choices that have specific examples.

<u>Example</u>: Noting that all choices are true, what is visible ..

Underline visible. Visible means something that can be discerned by the naked eye. Look for choices that talk about items that are visual or items that can be identified by the naked eye.

<u>Example</u>: Noting that all choices are true, what is clear ..

Underline clear. Clear means specific and not vague. Look for choices that give concrete examples or more specifics, and eliminate choices that talk about general recommendations or choices with no details.

In summary, these are the most common patterns in the test. Recognizing the patterns will help you improve your score by improving your accuracy and by improving your time management skills.

Here are the patterns:

Pattern	What to Do?
Pattern 1 – Transitional Phrases	• Eliminate choices by recognizing similar transitional phrases. • Always read the previous sentence together with the current sentence to confirm your answer.
Pattern 2 – Redundancy or Wordiness	• Eliminate choices that are wordy or have redundant phrases. Simple is better.
Pattern 3 – Subject Verb Agreement	• Identify the subject and the verb. • If possible, remove unnecessary information or qualifier; qualifier does not matter.
Pattern 4 – Subject Pronoun Agreement	• Identify the subject and the pronoun. • Make sure pronoun reference is crystal clear.
Pattern 5 – Who vs Whom & Whoever vs Whomever	• Identify this pattern when the choices have who and whom. • Who & whoever are needed when modifying subjects and whom & whomever are needed when modifying objects.
Pattern 6 – Punctuation	• Master the punctuation rules. Note the difference between an independent clause, dependent clause or sentence fragment and a run-on sentence. • Period and semicolon are interchangeable in that they separate two independent sentences. • Comma separates an independent sentence and a fragment. • Sentence before a colon should be an independent sentence. Colon can introduce a list with only one item. • One dash is used as a definition.
Pattern 7 – Title and Subject	• Title and Subject do not need commas in between.
Pattern 8 – Exceptions of Possessive Case	• Its means possessive. It's means "It is." • Plural subjects take apostrophe but no "s." Example: Jones' house, and not Jones's house.
Pattern 9 – Reflexive Pronoun	• No comma is needed between the subject and a reflexive pronoun. "He himself" and not "he, himself."
Pattern 10 – Use of Two Commas or Two Dashes or Two Parentheses	• What is between two commas or two dashes or two parentheses is optional and can be taken out to simplify the sentence.

Pattern 11 – Adjectives and Adverbs	• Adjectives modify nouns or pronouns and adverbs modify verbs, adverbs and adjectives. • The question type can be identified when you notice two choices that start with an adjective and two other choices that start with an adverb.
Pattern 12 – Adjective Phrase or Participle Phrase	• Make sure what comes after an adjective phrase is the noun that it intends to modify.
Pattern 13 – Parallel Structure	• Maintain parallel structure in a sentence to keep it consistent.
Pattern 14 – Faulty Comparison or Illogical Comparison	• Make sure items being compared are of the same type (like objects).
Pattern 15 – Verb Tense	• Identify first that it is a verb tense pattern by noting that the choices are using verbs. • Try to match the narration.
Pattern 16 – YES- or NO-type Questions	• Recognize the pattern first. • Decide to answer YES or NO. • Read only two choices that are relevant.
Pattern 17 – Underline Questions	• Underline key words or phrases in the question. • Look for answer choices that support these key words or phrases in the question. • Eliminate choices that are not answering the questions as it relates to the key underlined words or phrases.

4. General Test Taking Tips

1. Eliminate choices that mean the same or are essentially the same. Recognize there is only one correct answer. If there are several choices that mean the same, these choices cannot be simultaneously correct. Hence, you can eliminate them.
   a. This technique is especially helpful for questions involving transitional phrases.

2. Read all choices before picking your answer. You need to select the best choice.

3. Look before and after the current sentence. You will use this technique in several question types.
   a. If the question is about inserting or deleting the preceding or next sentence, read both previous and next sentences.
   b. Questions involving transitional phrases require you to read the previous sentence.
   c. Questions involving verb tense can be answered by reading the narration or by looking at the previous or next sentence.

4. Underline, circle, or remove information to simplify a sentence.
   a. Use this technique to focus on the subject when subject is followed by a qualifier. The qualifier is irrelevant. Hence, underline or circle or remove the qualifier to bring the subject and verb together.
   b. Questions involving two commas, two dashes or two parentheses can be simplified by removing the information within the two commas or two dashes or two parentheses.

5. Where to insert or delete
   a. Substituting each choice is useful for questions involving inserting and deleting a sentence. In addition, make sure to verify all choices.
   b. Questions involving where to insert or delete can be answered by reading the narration. Focus on what key information is added or deleted when inserting or deleting the sentence.

6. Looking at the narration is useful to answer questions involving verb tense.

7. Paying attention to what is underlined and what is not underlined is important.

8. Questions involving "EXCEPT," "NOT ACCEPTABLE" or "LEAST ACCEPTABLE" should be handled carefully. Underline the phrase "EXCEPT" or "NOT ACCEPTABLE" to avoid making a mistake.

5. Practice Questions

For the following practice problems, first identify the concept being tested. Refer to the pages where a summary of question patterns was included. After you identify the pattern, select the best answer choice.

1. The local newspaper article recognized John for his <u>outstanding achievement</u>.
   - A. NO CHANGE.
   - B. outstandingly achievement
   - C. outstandingly achieve
   - D. outstanding achieving

Concept	Pattern 11, Adjectives and Adverbs. Choice A.

2. To the jubilation of <u>it's</u> fans, the team won the championship.
   - A. NO CHANGE
   - B. its'
   - C. its
   - D. their

Concept	Pattern 8, Exceptions of Possessive Case. Choice C.

3. It was <u>raining, therefore,</u> we stayed home.
   - A. NO CHANGE
   - B. raining. Therefore,
   - C. raining, therefore
   - D. raining: therefore,

Concept	

4. The neighborhood has many poor students, <u>several of those</u> are unable to afford basic education.
   - A. NO CHANGE
   - B. several of whom
   - C. several of who
   - D. several of which

Concept	

5. <u>He, himself</u> solved the long-standing mystery.
   - A. NO CHANGE
   - B. He himself,
   - C. He, himself,
   - D. He himself

Concept	

6. The flight leaves <u>at 6 a.m., in the morning.</u>
   - A. NO CHANGE
   - B. at 6 a.m. in the morning.
   - C. in the early morning at 6 a.m.
   - D. at 6 a.m.

Concept	

7. I like <u>Britney Spears' songs better than Selena Gomez</u>.
  - A. NO CHANGE
  - B. Britney Spears's songs better than Selena Gomez's songs.
  - C. Britney Spears's songs better than Selena Gomez.
  - (D.) Britney Spears' songs better than Selena Gomez's songs.

Concept	

8. This proposal is between <u>you and I</u>.
  - A. NO CHANGE
  - (B.) you and me.
  - C. you and mine.
  - D. your and me.

Concept	

9. The new CEO implemented many programs to cut costs. <u>As a result</u>, the company was able to pay higher dividends this year.
  - (A.) NO CHANGE
  - B. Conversely
  - C. On the other hand
  - D. Alternatively

Concept	

10. <u>The Jones house</u> is on the market.
  - A. NO CHANGE
  - (B.) Jones' house
  - C. Jones house's
  - (D.) Jones's house

Concept	

11. <u>The architectural elements of the new building was</u> attracting many visitors.
  - A. NO CHANGE
  - B. The architectural elements of the new building is
  - C. The architectural elements of the new building has
  - (D.) The architectural elements of the new building are

Concept	

12. Coach, William was responsible for many championships at our high school.
    A. NO CHANGE
    B. Coach William,
    C. Coach, William,
    D. Coach William ⃝

Concept	

13. India's weather is hotter than Germany.
    A. NO CHANGE ⃝
    B. India's weather is hotter than Germany's weather.
    C. India is hotter than Germany's weather.
    D. India's weather is hottest of the two.

Concept	

14. It was raining, however, we continued to play outdoors.
    A. NO CHANGE ⃝
    B. raining. However,
    C. raining, However
    D. raining however,

Concept	

15. For who did you vote?
    A. NO CHANGE
    B. whom ⃝
    C. whose
    D. which

Concept	

16. After deliberating for several days, the verdict was given by the jury.
    A. NO CHANGE ⃝
    B. After deliberating for several days, the verdict was given.
    C. After deliberating for several days, the jury gave the verdict.
    D. After deliberation for several days, the verdict was arrived at.

Concept	

17. The advertisements in the 1930s are not similar to the 1980s.
    A. NO CHANGE ⃝
    B. The advertisements in the 1930s are not the same as the 1980s.
    C. The advertisements in the 1930s are not as in the 1980s.
    D. The advertisements in the 1930s are not the same as the advertisements in the 1980s.

27

$$\frac{2\sqrt{3}}{\sqrt{3}} \cdot \frac{\sqrt{3}}{\sqrt{3}} \quad \frac{2\sqrt{3}}{3} \quad \frac{1}{\sqrt{3}} \cdot \frac{\sqrt{3}}{\sqrt{3}} = \frac{\sqrt{3}}{3}$$

Concept	

18. John practiced for long hours and enjoy the success.
    A. NO CHANGE
    B. John practiced for long hours and enjoying the success.
    C. John practiced for long hours and enjoyed the success.
    D. John practicing for long hours and enjoyed the success.

Concept	

19. Rachel told Mom that she needs to see a doctor.
    A. NO CHANGE   B. Rachel needs
    C. she need   D. Rachel need

Concept	

20. Which of the following is NOT acceptable.
    A. We went to the airport early. However, the flight was delayed.
    B. We went to the airport early; however, the flight was delayed.
    C. We went to the airport early, the flight was delayed.
    D. We went to the airport early and found that the flight was delayed.

Concept	

21. She, herself was cleaning the house.
    A. NO CHANGE   B. She herself
    C. She herself,   D. She, herself,

Concept	

22. He wondered about who the plot was.
    A. NO CHANGE   B. whoever
    C. whom   D. whose

Concept	

23. I am capricious, on the other hand, my brother is thoughtful.
    A. NO CHANGE   B. capricious, on the other hand
    C. capricious. On the other hand,   D. capricious, on the other hand.

28

Concept	

24. This medicine is for <u>she and I.</u>
    - A. NO CHANGE
    - B. she and me.
    - C. her and I.
    - (D.) her and me.

Concept	

25. Teaching is fun. <u>Conversely,</u> teaching helps me learn from my students.
    - A. NO CHANGE
    - B. However,
    - C. On the other hand,
    - (D.) Moreover,

Concept	

26. Finding a good partner is like <u>someone</u> winning a lottery.
    - A. NO CHANGE
    - B. somebody
    - C. a person
    - (D.) DELETE the underlined portion.

Concept	

27. <u>The United States's stance</u> on the issue is understandable.
    - A. NO CHANGE
    - (B.) The United State's stance
    - C. The United States stance
    - D. The United States' stance

Concept	

28. <u>Magician, Blaine,</u> mesmerized all of us with his astounding magic tricks.
    - A. NO CHANGE
    - (B.) Magician Blaine
    - C. Magician, Blaine
    - D. Magician Blaine,

Concept	

29. The United States has one unique <u>feature; its diversity.</u>
    - A. NO CHANGE
    - B. feature. Its diversity.
    - C. feature, that is, its diversity
    - (D.) feature: its diversity.

Concept	

30. There are no secrets between <u>you and I.</u>
    A. NO CHANGE
    B. you and mine.
    C. you or I
    D. you and me.

Concept	

31. After many deliberations, the jury reached <u>a decision, not guilty.</u>
    A. NO CHANGE
    B. a decision. Not guilty.
    C. a decision: not guilty.
    D. a decision; not guilty.

Concept	

32. <u>Who</u> did you meet at the dinner last night?
    A. NO CHANGE
    B. Which
    C. Whoever
    D. Whom

Concept	

33. The president, along with his team, <u>is planning to</u> visit China.
    A. NO CHANGE
    B. are planning to
    C. is plan to
    D. are plan to

Concept	

34. <u>The most unique ability</u> of this artist is his ability to understand the pulse of his audience.
    A. NO CHANGE
    B. The unique ability
    C. The most unique abilities
    D. The unique abilities

Concept	

35. After taking office, the new president <u>reverted back</u> the policies of the previous government.
    A. NO CHANGE
    B. revert back
    C. reverted
    D. reverted out

Concept	

36. <u>Somebody left their</u> belongings in the class.
    A. NO CHANGE
    B. Someone left theirs
    C. Somebody left his or her
    D. Someone left their's

Concept	

37. Skiing is exciting. <u>In addition</u>, skiing can lead to serious injuries.
- A. NO CHANGE
- B. Besides
- C. Moreover
- D. However

Concept	

38. You know what to <u>do, practice every day</u>.
- A. NO CHANGE
- B. do: practice every day.
- C. do. Practicing every day.
- D. do; practicing every day.

Concept	

39. John is <u>who</u> I think is visiting us tomorrow.
- A. NO CHANGE
- B. whom
- C. whose
- D. which

Concept	

40. <u>The book discussed three forms of Indian dance: Kathakali, Kuchipudi and Bharat Natyam.</u>
- A. NO CHANGE
- B. The book discussed three forms of Indian dance; Kathakali, Kuchipudi and Bharat Natyam.
- C. The book discussed three forms of Indian dance – Kathakali, Kuchipudi and Bharat Natyam.
- D. The book discussed Indian dance, three forms of which are Kathakali, Kuchipudi and Bharat Natyam.

Concept	

41. <u>Paris's new mayor</u> announced several reforms.
- A. NO CHANGE
- B. Paris new mayor
- C. Paris' new mayor
- D. Paris's' new mayor

Concept	

42. The government banned <u>not only pubic smoking but also litter in the parks.</u>
- A. NO CHANGE
- B. not only smoke publicly but also littering in the parks.
- C. not only public smoking but also littering in the parks.

D.   not only public smoking and littering in the parks.

Concept	

43. Many of her exhibits in this realm attract students and teachers alike.
    A. NO CHANGE   B. Each
    C. Everyone   D. One

Concept	

44. Mary got what she worked for: an admission to Stanford College of Business.
    A. NO CHANGE   B. for, an admission
    C. for; an admission   D. for. An admission

Concept	

45. To who did you deliver the presents yesterday?
    A. NO CHANGE   B. whom
    C. whose   D. which

Concept	

46. Everybody is wearing their hats and uniforms at the parade.
    A. NO CHANGE   B. his or her hats and uniforms
    C. their hat and uniform   D. his or her hat and uniform

Concept	

47. I love traveling to new places. Conversely, I enjoy travelling in Asia.
    A. NO CHANGE   B. However,
    C. Specifically,   D. On the contrary,

Concept	

48. Elegantly models walked the runway.
    A. NO CHANGE   B. Elegantly models walk the runway.
    C. Elegant models walked the runway. D. Elegant models walking the runway.

Concept	

49. I like playing outdoor sports. <u>Conversely,</u> I like playing tennis.
   A. NO CHANGE
   B. In particular,
   C. On the other hand,
   D. However,

Concept	

50. Finally, I am delighted to meet my long-time mentor <u>who</u> helped me get through college.
   A. NO CHANGE
   B. whom
   C. whose
   D. which

Concept	

51. My dad gave me the best rule to live <u>by, work hard.</u>
   A. NO CHANGE
   B. by: work hard.
   C. by; work hard.
   D. by. work hard.

Concept	

52. The committee, hailed as the most meaningful improvement in the election laws, <u>were instrumental</u> in the passage of the new legislation.
   A. NO CHANGE
   B. is instrumental
   C. was instrumental
   D. was instrumentally

Concept	

53. <u>Long held in high esteem among the selection panel, rumor has it that Michael is quitting the sport.</u>
   A. NO CHANGE
   B. <u>Long held in high esteem among the selection panel, it is rumored that Michael is quitting the sport.</u>
   C. <u>Long held in high esteem among the selection panel, Michael has been rumored to be quitting the sport.</u>
   D. <u>Long held in high esteem among the selection panel, it is rumored that Michael will be quitting the sport.</u>

Concept	

54. The president had one underline{message: serve} your country.
   A. NO CHANGE
   B. message, serve
   C. message. Serving
   D. message; serving

Concept	

55. I enjoy visiting national monuments. underline{Conversely,} Mt.Rushmore is my favorite.
   A. NO CHANGE
   B. However,
   C. On the other hand,
   D. In particular,

Concept	

56. The professionals who interact with the underline{government makes} sure the issues are resolved in a timely manner.
   A. NO CHANGE
   B. government make
   C. government making
   D. government is making

Concept	

57. underline{Citing the Scientology Program, it helped Thomas get through a very challenging period in his life}.
   A. NO CHANGE
   B. Citing the Scientology Program, Thomas thinks the program helped him get through a very challenging period in his life.
   C. Citing the Scientology Program, the program helped Thomas get through a very challenging period in his life.
   D. Citing the Scientology Program, a very challenging period in his life was overcome by Thomas.

Concept	

58. The congress elected by the underline{citizens were} instrumental in the passage of the new legislation.
   A. NO CHANGE
   B. citizen is
   C. citizens are
   D. citizens is

Concept	

59. underline{Although} I like playing outdoor sports, I also enjoy playing racquetball.
   A. NO CHANGE
   B. Because
   C. Due to the fact that
   D. As a result of

Concept	

60. Nobody is going to give their secrets away in this business.
   A. NO CHANGE
   B. their secrets away in their business.
   C. his or her secrets away in the business.
   D. their secrets away in their businesses.

Concept	

61. With whom are you going to the prom tomorrow?
   A. NO CHANGE
   B. who
   C. whoever
   D. whomever

Concept	

62. As an evangelical follower, Mary continues to participate in many activities at the church.
   A. NO CHANGE
   B. As an evangelical follower, the church has seen Mary participate in many activities.
   C. As an evangelical follower, many activities were participated by Mary at the church.
   D. As an evangelical follower, the church welcomed Mary's participation in many activities.

Concept	

63. The city officials of the Indian community acts in the interest of the community.
   A. NO CHANGE
   B. community act
   C. communities acts
   D. communities acting

Concept	

64. As a lead singer in the band, Britney's concerts attracted a large audience.
   A. NO CHANGE
   B. As a lead singer in the band, a large audience are attracted by Britney's concerts.
   C. As a lead singer in the band, a large audience is attracted by Britney's concerpts.
   D. As a lead singer in the band, Britney attracted a large audience at her concerts.

Concept	

65. Movements of tectonic plates create volcanoes along the plate boundaries, which erupt and _forms_ mountains.

    A. NO CHANGE

    C. formed

    B. forming

    D. form

Concept	

66. All mountain chains on the face of the _planet, without exception, are the result of tectonic plate movement_.

    A. NO CHANGE

    B. planet, without exception, is the result of tectonic plate movement.

    C. planet, without exceptions, are the result of tectonic plate movement.

    D. planet, without exception, is formed as a result of tectonic plate movement.

Concept	

67. As expected, Bolt _– fastest man on earth,_ won the gold medal.

    B. NO CHANGE

    C. – fastest man on earth –

    B. fastest man on earth –

    D. fastest man on earth,

Concept	

68. Give the invitation to _whom_ you please.

    A. NO CHANGE

    C. who

    B. whomever

    D. whoever

Concept	

69. Because of the president's meaningless policies, his impeachment is _imminent and can happen in the near future._

    A. NO CHANGE

    C. imminent and happen soon.

    B. imminent.

    D. imminent and likely to happen soon.

Concept	

70. _Inadvertently and unintentionally,_ I sent the payment to the wrong vendor.

    A. NO CHANGE

    C. Inadvertently

    B. Inadvertently and accidently

    D. Accidently and unintentionally

Concept	

71. Asked about her divorce with Brad, the reporter was requested to respect Angelina's privacy.

   A. NO CHANGE

   B. Asked about her divorse with Brad, the reporter was requested to respect her privacy.

   C. Asked about her divorce with Brad, Angelina requested the reporter respect her privacy.

   D. Asked about her divorce with Brad, her privacy was requested to be respected by the reporter.

Concept	

72. Columbus's first landfall in the New World was on an island named San Salvador.

   A. NO CHANGE   B. Columbus

   C. Columbus'   D. Columbus is

Concept	

73. To everyone's dismay, John – tardiest employee of all – showed up on time.

   A. NO CHANGE   B. tardiest employee of all,

   C. tardiest employee of all;   D. tardiest employee of all:

Concept	

74. Although Einstein's Theory of Relativity is difficult to read, it is very interesting.

   A. NO CHANGE   B. For example,

   C. Likewise,   D. For instance,

Concept	

75. I met Mr. Smith – my son's chess coach, at the tournament.

   A. NO CHANGE   B. my son's chess coach –

   C. my son's chess coach,   D. – my son's chess coach –

Concept	

76. Bobby Fisher was focused on one thing: winning the game.

   A. NO CHANGE   B. on one thing. Winning

   C. on one thing; winning   D. on one thing, winning

Concept	

77. I don't know <u>who</u> you are inviting to the graduation party next week.
    A. NO CHANGE   (B.) whom
    C. which   D. whoever

Concept	

78. <u>Known for his bold roles, Anthony was nominated for the Oscar for his recent movie, "Cannibal."</u>
    (A.) NO CHANGE
    B. Known for his bold roles, Oscar nomination was submitted for Anthony for his recent movie, "Cannibal."
    C. Known for his bold roles, recent movie of Anthony, "Cannibal," received an Oscar nomination.
    D. Known for his bold roles, "Cannibal," a recent movie of Anthony received an Oscar nomination.

Concept	

79. Home to over 500 beautiful islands, the archipelago of the Bahamas <u>lies</u> southwest off the coast of Florida.
    (A.) NO CHANGE   B. lie
    C. lay   D. laying

Concept	

80. The baby elephant is trying to stand on <u>it's</u> legs.
    A. NO CHANGE   B. its'
    (C.) its   D. their

Concept	

81. The technology company launched a <u>new and improved</u> mobile phone.
    (A.) NO CHANGE   B. new and improved version of the
    C. latest and improved   D. new

Concept	

82. <u>Bahamas's beaches are known for their spectacular beauty.</u>
    A. NO CHANGE
    (B.) Bahamas' beaches are known for their spectacular beauty.
    C. Bahamas' beaches are known for its spectacular beauty.

D. Bahamas's beaches are known for its spectacular beauty.

Concept	

83. Please call my doctor <u>Joe Williams,</u> tomorrow.
    A. NO CHANGE   B. – Joe Williams –
    C. Joe Williams –,   D. – Joe Williams,

Concept	

84. <u>Being that</u> he was driven to succeed as a cricket player, Sachin practiced a lot.
    A. NO CHANGE   B. Because
    C. Due to the fact that   D. As a result of his desire that

Concept	

85. <u>Co-starring alongside Tommy, one of his best performances in the movie, "The Fugitive," was produced by Harrison.</u>
    A. NO CHANGE
    B. <u>Co-starring alongside Tommy, Harrison produced one of his best performances in the movie, "The Fugitive."</u>
    C. <u>Co-starring alongside Tommy, the movie, "The Fugitive," saw one of his best performances by Harrison.</u>
    D. <u>Co-starring alongside Tommy, "The Fugitive" movie produced one of Harrison's best performances.</u>

Concept	

86. Mary told me <u>who</u> to contact once I reach the city.
    A. NO CHANGE   B. whom
    C. whose   D. whoever

Concept	

87. This restaurant serves authentic India food. <u>Conversely,</u> this is the best restaurant in town.
    A. NO CHANGE   B. However,
    C. On the other hand,   D. In fact,

Concept	

88. <u>Cyprus's</u> standard of living is reflected in the country's very high human development index.

    Ⓐ NO CHANGE   B. Cyprus'

    C. Cyprus   D. Cyprus's is

Concept	

89. <u>Nominated for her role in the movie "Love in Singapore," a black Valentino gown with long sleeves, a high neck and floor-length skirt was worn by Nicole.</u>

    Ⓐ NO CHANGE

    B. <u>Nominated for her role in the movie "Love in Singapore," a black Valentino gown with long sleeves, a high neck and floor-length skirt was what Nicole wore.</u>

    C. <u>Nominated for her role in the movie "Love in Singapore," Nicole wore a black Valentino gown with long sleeves, a high neck and floor-length skirt.</u>

    D. <u>Nominated for her role in the movie "Love in Singapore," a black Valentino gown with long sleeves, a high neck and floor-length skirt was Nicole's dress.</u>

Concept	

90. <u>General Dynamics's profits</u> are declining due to poor management and leadership.

    A. NO CHANGE   Ⓑ General Dynamics' profit

    C. General Dynamics' profits   D. General Dynamics profits

Concept	

91. Students are required to attend all classes. <u>On the other hand,</u> they are required to complete homework every week.

    A. NO CHANGE   B. However,

    C. Conversely,   Ⓓ In Fact,

Concept	

92. I am not sure <u>who</u> to trust anymore.

    A. NO CHANGE   Ⓑ whom

    C. which to   D. whose

Concept	

93. My math book has 200 pages; in addition, my English book has only 100 pages.
   A. NO CHANGE   B. however,
   C. moreover,   D. additionally,

Concept	

94. If you need something, call my manager – John, not Joe, and he will help you.
   A. NO CHANGE   B. – John, not Joe –
   C. : John, not Joe,   D. , John, not Joe –

Concept	

95. Finally, the college basketball team lost it's winning streak.
   A. NO CHANGE   B. its
   C. its'   D. their

Concept	

96. Jobs are coming back to the United States by virtue of the fact that our economy is improving.
   A. NO CHANGE   B. because
   C. as a result of the fact that D. due to the fact that

Concept	

97. I visited many national parks. For example, I visited Mt. Rushmore, Yellowstone, Yosemite, Grand Canyon and Zion National Parks.
   A. NO CHANGE   B. In addition,
   C. On the other hand,   D. Moreover,

Concept	

98. They are constantly working on new innovations in cyber security.
   A. NO CHANGE   B. newer innovations
   C. innovations   D. new inventions

Concept	

99. Despite Anand's elaborate preparations, he lost to Kasparov.
   A. NO CHANGE   B. Because of
   C. As a result of   D. Due to

Concept	

100. Given our <u>past history,</u> we should set clear expectations.
- (A) NO CHANGE
- B. prior history,
- C. history in the past,
- D. history,

Concept	

101. Chess requires much practice and skill. <u>Conversely,</u> mountain climbing requires a lot of practice.
- A. NO CHANGE
- B. However,
- C. On the other hand,
- (D.) Similarly,

Concept	

102. Due to overwhelming customer feedback, the company <u>reverted back</u> to the previous version.
- A. NO CHANGE
- (B.) reverted
- C. reverted the product back
- D. went back in reverse

Concept	

103. The chairperson is ill. <u>Conversely,</u> the committee is not meeting tomorrow.
- A. NO CHANGE
- B. However,
- C. On the other hand,
- (D.) Thus,

Concept	

104. John lost his job last month. <u>Conversely,</u> he is not able to pay his bills.
- A. NO CHANGE
- B. However,
- C. On the other hand,
- (D.) Therefore,

Concept	

105. <u>At first,</u> I initially was afraid of bungee-jumping.
- A. NO CHANGE
- B. First
- C. Firstly
- (D.) Delete the underlined words

Concept	

106. It rained <u>consecutively</u> for ten days.
- A. NO CHANGE
- B. nonstop
- C. Consecutively nonstop
- D. Delete the underlined word

Concept	

107. The first time I went out of the country <u>– and to the United States –</u> was to attend graduate school.
- A. NO CHANGE
- B. and to the United States –
- C. and to the United States;
- D. and to the United States,

Concept	

108. The city lost <u>its'</u> old appeal.
- A. NO CHANGE
- B. it's
- C. its
- D. their

Concept	

6. Solutions to Practice Questions

1. ***Best answer is A.*** Concept being tested is <u>Adjectives and Adverbs, Pattern 11</u>. Adverbs modify verbs, adverbs and adjectives whereas adjectives modify nouns and pronouns. *Achievement* is a noun. What type of achievement is it? It is an *outstanding* achievement. Choices B and C use adverbs. Choice D has incorrect verb form *achieving*.

2. ***Best answer is C.*** Concept being tested is the <u>Exceptions of Possessive Case, Pattern 8</u>. It's means "It is." Hence, choice A is incorrect. Choice B is not a proper English phrase. Choice D introduces a plural, "their." Team is singular. Hence, "its" is appropriate. No apostrophe needed.

3. ***Best answer is B.*** Concept being tested is <u>Punctuation, Pattern 6</u>. Choices A and C are wrong because a comma cannot separate two independent clauses. Choice D is incorrect usage of a colon. Choice B correctly separates two independent clauses with a period.

4. ***Best answer is B.*** Concept being tested is <u>Who vs Whom & Whoever vs Whomever, Pattern 5</u>. Who is used when a subject is needed. Whom is used when an object is needed. "Of" is a preposition and hence, it needs an object. "several of whom" is correct.

5. ***Best answer is D.*** Concept being tested is <u>Reflexive Pronoun, Pattern 9</u>. Keep reflexive pronoun and the subject together. No comma is needed to separate the subject and the reflexive pronoun. Pick a choice that has no commas at all.

6. ***Best answer is D.*** Concept being tested is <u>Redundancy or Wordiness, Pattern 2</u>. "a.m." and "in the morning" are redundant. Choice D eliminates the redundancy.

7. ***Best answer is D.*** Concepts being tested are <u>Exceptions of Possessive Case, Pattern 8 and Faulty Comparison or Illogical Comparison, Pattern 14</u>. For nouns ending in "s," apostrophe is *not* followed by "s." Hence, choice B is incorrect. In addition, Britney's songs should be compared to Selena's songs. Choices A and C incorrectly compare Britney's songs with Selena Gomez, i.e. songs are compared to a person.

8. ***Best answer is B.*** Concept being tested is <u>Subject Pronoun Agreement, Pattern 4</u>. "Between" is a preposition. Prepositions take objects. Hence, "between you and I" is incorrect. Correct usage is "between you and me."

9. ***Best answer is A.*** Concept being tested is <u>Transitional Phrases, Pattern 1</u>. Read the previous sentence. It implies that the company was able to pay the dividends because of the cost cutting measures taken by the new CEO. Choices B, C and D do not imply affirmation; instead, they imply opposition.

10. ***Best answer is B.*** Concept being tested is <u>Exceptions of Possessive Case, Pattern 8</u>. Choice D is not proper English. Choice C incorrectly places the apostrophe after house. Choice A does not even indicate a possessive case. For nouns ending in s, no "s" is needed after the apostrophe. Choice B correctly indicates possessive form of nouns ending in s.

11. ***Best answer is D.*** Concept being tested is <u>Subject Verb Agreement, Pattern 3</u>. "Elements" is the subject of the sentence. Subject is plural and hence, you need a plural verb, "are." Choices A, B and C introduce a singular verb. You can read the sentence by removing "of the new building" which is a qualifier. Read the sentence as *"The architectural elements are attracting many visitors."*

12. ***Best answer is D.*** Concept being tested is <u>Title and Subject, Pattern 7</u>. Title is part of the subject. Do not separate the title and subject with commas. Instead, keep the title and the subject together. Only Choice D has no commas.

13. ***Best answer is B.*** Concept being tested is <u>Faulty Comparison or Illogical Comparison, Pattern 14</u>. India's weather should be compared to Germany's weather. Choice A is incorrectly comparing India's weather to Germany. Choice C is comparing India to Germany's weather. In choice D, "hottest" is incorrect. When comparing two items, you should use "hotter" as in choice B.

14. ***Best answer is B.*** Concept being tested is <u>Punctuation, Pattern 6</u>. Choices A and C are ending the first sentence with a comma. Choice D does not have any punctuation after the first sentence making it a run-on sentence. Only choice B correctly separates both sentences with a period.

15. ***Best answer is B.*** Concept being tested is <u>Who vs Whom & Whoever vs Whomever, Pattern 5</u>. Who is used when a subject is needed. Whom is used when an object is needed. If the answer is him/her, "whom" is needed. If the answer is he/she, "who" is needed. You voted for *him/her*. Hence, *whom* is needed.

16. ***Best answer is C.*** Concept being tested is <u>Adjective Phrase or Participle Phrase, Pattern 12</u>. Adjective phrases modify the subject/noun that follows the phrase. Who deliberated for several days? The jury did. Hence, jury should follow the adjective phrase. Only choice C correctly introduces the subject after the adjective phrase.

17. ***Best answer is D.*** Concept being tested is <u>Faulty Comparison or Illogical Comparison, Pattern 14</u>. The advertisements in the 1930s should be compared to the advertisements in the 1980s. Only choice D makes the correct comparison.

18. ***Best answer is C.*** Concepts being tested are <u>Parallel Structure, Pattern 13 and Verb Tense, Pattern 15</u>. What did John do? John *practiced* for long hours and John *enjoyed* the success. "Practiced" and "enjoyed" should be of the same verb form.

19. ***Best answer is B.*** Concept being tested is <u>Subject Pronoun Agreement, Pattern 4</u>. Because both the subjects are feminine, it is not clear who "she" refers to. "She" could be referring to Rachel or Mom. Hence, "she" should be replaced with Rachel or Mom. In choice D, "need" is incorrect. Instead, it should say "Rachel needs" to see a doctor.

20. ***Best answer is C.*** Concept being tested is <u>Punctuation, Pattern 6</u>. Choices A and B correctly separate two independent clauses with a period and semicolon. Choice D separates the two sentences with a coordinated conjunction. Choice C incorrectly separates two sentences with a comma.

21. ***Best answer is B.*** Concept being tested is <u>Reflexive Pronoun, Pattern 9</u>. Keep the reflexive pronoun and the subject together. No comma is needed to separate the subject and the reflexive pronoun. Pick a choice that has no commas at all.

22. ***Best answer is C.*** Concept being tested is <u>Who vs Whom & Whoever vs Whomever, Pattern 5</u>. Who is used when a subject is needed. Whom is used when an object is needed. "About" is a preposition and it needs an object. In addition, you would say the plot was about *him/her*. Hence, *whom* is needed.

23. ***Best answer is C.*** Concept being tested is <u>Punctuation, Pattern 6</u>. Only choice C correctly separates both sentences with a period.

24. ***Best answer is D.*** Concept being tested is <u>Subject Pronoun Agreement, Pattern 4</u>. "For" is a preposition. A preposition takes an object. Hence, "for she and I" is incorrect. Correct usage is "for her and me."

25. ***Best answer is D.*** Concept being tested is <u>Transitional Phrases, Pattern 1</u>. Read the previous sentence. The two sentences are reinforcing in nature, not contradicting. Hence, choices A, B and C are incorrect. Choice D is the only one that is reinforcing.

26. ***Best answer is D.*** Concept being tested is <u>Parallel Structure, Pattern 13</u>. "Finding" and "winning" are the elements of the parallel structure. "Someone" is redundant and breaks the parallel structure. "Someone" can be deleted.

27. ***Best answer is D.*** Concept being tested is <u>Exceptions of Possessive Case, Pattern 8</u>. For nouns ending in "s," apostrophe is *not* followed by "s." Hence, choice A is incorrect. Choice B reads "United State," instead it should read "United States." Choice C is incorrect because it is missing an apostrophe. Choice D has an apostrophe but is not followed by an "s." Hence, choice D is the best choice.

28. ***Best answer is B.*** Concept being tested is <u>Title and Subject, Pattern 7</u>. Title is part of the subject. Do not separate the title and the subject with commas. Instead, keep the title and the subject together. Only choice B has no commas.

29. ***Best answer is D.*** Concept being tested is <u>Punctuation, Pattern 6</u>. Note that in choices A and B, "its diversity" is not an independent clause. Hence, a period and a semicolon are not appropriate. Choice C is using commas to separate two independent clauses. Choice D is correct. The sentence before a colon is an independent clause. Colon is introducing a list. In this instance, the list has only one item, i.e. "its diversity."

30. ***Best answer is D.*** Concept being tested is <u>Subject Pronoun Agreement, Pattern 4</u>. "Between" is a preposition. A preposition takes an object. Hence, "between you and I" is incorrect. Correct usage is "between you and me."

31. ***Best answer is C.*** Concept being tested is <u>Punctuation, Pattern 6</u>. Note that in choices B and D, "not guilty" is not an independent clause. Hence, a period and a semicolon are not appropriate. Choice A is using commas to separate two independent clauses. Choice C is correct. The sentence

before a colon is an independent clause. Colon is introducing a list. In this instance, the list has only one item, i.e. "not guilty."

32. **Best answer is D.** Concept being tested is <u>Who vs Whom & Whoever vs Whomever, Pattern 5</u>. Who is used when a subject is needed. Whom is used when an object is needed. In this case, you would answer the question with a *him/her*. I met *him/her* at the dinner. Hence, *whom* is needed.

33. **Best answer is A.** Concept being tested is <u>Subject Verb Agreement, Pattern 3</u>. "President" is the subject of the sentence. Subject is singular and hence, it needs a singular verb, "is." Choices B and D introduce a plural verb. Choice C uses incorrect verb form. You can read the sentence by removing "along with his team" which is a qualifier. The sentence should read as *"The president is planning to visit China."*

34. **Best answer is B.** Concept being tested is <u>Redundancy or Wordiness, Pattern 2</u>. "Unique" means rare. Hence, it is incorrect to say "the most unique ability." Choice B eliminates the redundancy.

35. **Best answer is C.** Concept being tested is <u>Redundancy or Wordiness, Pattern 2</u>. "Revert" means "taking something back." Hence, it is incorrect to say "revert back." Choice C eliminates the redundancy.

36. **Best answer is C.** Concept being tested is <u>Subject Pronoun Agreement, Pattern 4</u>. "Somebody" is singular. Remember, "<u>body</u>" not bodies. On the other hand, "their" is plural. Hence, choices A, B and D are incorrect. Choice C matches singular subject with singular pronoun.

37. **Best answer is D.** Concept being tested is <u>Transitional Phrases, Pattern 1</u>. Read the previous sentence. The two sentences are contrasting in nature. Hence, choices A, B and C are incorrect. Choice D is the only one that is introducing a contrast.

38. **Best answer is B.** Concept being tested is <u>Punctuation, Pattern 6</u>. Note that in choices C and D, "practice every day" is not an independent clause. Hence, a period and a semicolon are not appropriate. Choice A is using a comma. Choice B is correct. The sentence before a colon is an independent clause. Colon is introducing a list. In this instance, the list has only one item, i.e. "practice every day."

39. **Best answer is A.** Concept being tested is <u>Who vs Whom & Whoever vs Whomever, Pattern 5</u>. Who is used when a subject is needed. Whom is used when an object is needed. John is coming to the dinner. Hence, *who* is needed.

40. **Best answer is A.** Concept being tested is <u>Punctuation, Pattern 6</u>. This is a correct usage of a colon. Colon introduces a list. In this case, there are three items in the list. In addition, the sentence before the colon is an independent clause.

41. **Best answer is C.** Concept being tested is <u>Exceptions of Possessive Case, Pattern 8</u>. Choice D is not proper English. Choice B does not even indicate a possessive case. For nouns ending in s, no "s" is needed after the apostrophe. Hence, choice A is incorrect. Choice C is the correct possessive form involving a noun ending in s.

42. **Best answer is C.** Concept being tested is Parallel Structure, Pattern 13. The government banned two things. The government banned public smoking. The government banned littering in the parks. Choices A and B break the parallel structure by mixing up the verb tense. Choice D is incorrect because "not only" should be followed by "but also."

43. **Best answer is A.** Concept being tested is Subject Verb Agreement, Pattern 3. The verb in the sentence is "*attract,*" which is plural and hence, it needs a plural subject. Only choice A introduces plural subject. Everyone, each and one are singular subjects. *Many* of her exhibits *attract* students.

44. **Best answer is A.** Concept being tested is Punctuation, Pattern 6. Note that in choices C and D, "an admission to Stanford College of Business" is not an independent clause. Hence, a period and a semicolon are not appropriate. Choice B is incorrectly using a comma. Choice A is correct. The sentence before a colon is an independent clause. Colon is introducing a list. In this instance, the list has only one item, i.e. "an admission to Stanford College of Business."

45. **Best answer is B.** Concept being tested is Who vs Whom & Whoever vs Whomever, Pattern 5. Who is used when a subject is needed. Whom is used when an object is needed. In this case, you would answer the question with a *him/her*. I delivered the presents to him/her. Hence, *whom* is needed.

46. **Best answer is D.** Concept being tested is Subject Pronoun Agreement, Pattern 4. The subject is "everybody." Every*body* is singular (not bodies). Hence, it requires a singular pronoun. Choices A and C can be eliminated. Choice B is incorrect because "hats" and "uniforms" are plural. A person is wearing one hat and one uniform, not many hats and many uniforms at one time. Hence, choice D is correct.

47. **Best answer is C.** Concept being tested is Transitional Phrases, Pattern 1. Traveling to Asia is an example. Read the previous sentence. The two sentences are reinforcing in nature, not contradicting. Hence, choices A, B and D are incorrect. Choice C is the only one that is reinforcing in nature.

48. **Best answer is C.** Concept being tested is Adjectives and Adverbs, Pattern 11. Adverbs modify verbs, adverbs and adjectives where as adjectives modify nouns and pronouns. "Models" is a noun. What type of models? Elegant models. Choices A and B use adverbs. Choice D has incorrect verb form "walking."

49. **Best answer is B.** Concept being tested is Transitional Phrases, Pattern 1. Tennis is an outdoor sport. Read the previous sentence. The two sentences are reinforcing in nature, not contradicting. Hence, choices A, C and D are incorrect. Choice B is the only one that is reinforcing in nature.

50. **Best answer is A.** Concept being tested is Who vs Whom & Whoever vs Whomever, Pattern 5. Who is used when a subject is needed. Whom is used when an object is needed. In this case, you would answer the question with a *he/she*. He/she helped me get through college. Hence, *who* is needed.

51. **Best answer is B.** Concept being tested is Punctuation, Pattern 6. Note that in choices C and D, "work hard" is not an independent clause. Hence, a period and a semicolon are not appropriate.

Choice A is incorrectly using a comma. Choice B is correct. The sentence before a colon is an independent clause. Colon is introducing a list. In this instance, the list has only one item, i.e. "work hard."

52. **Best answer is C.** Concept being tested is <u>Subject Verb Agreement, Pattern 3</u>. "Committee" is the subject of the sentence. The subject is singular and hence, it needs a singular verb. Legislation was already passed. Hence, "was" is appropriate.

53. **Best answer is C.** Concept being tested is <u>Adjective Phrase or Participle Phrase, Pattern 12</u>. Adjective phrases modify the subject/noun that follows the phrase. Who was held in high esteem? Michael was. Hence, the adjective phrase should be immediately followed by Michael. Only choice C introduces Michael right after the adjective clause.

54. **Best answer is A.** Concept being tested is <u>Punctuation, Pattern 6</u>. Note that in choices C and D, "serve your country" is not an independent clause. Hence, a period and a semicolon are not appropriate. Choice B is incorrectly using a comma. Choice A is correct. The sentence before a colon is an independent clause. Colon is introducing a list. In this instance, the list has only one item, i.e. "serve your country."

55. **Best answer is D.** Concept being tested is <u>Transitional Phrases, Pattern 1</u>. Mt. Rushmore is a national monument. Read the previous sentence. Two sentences are reinforcing in nature, not contradicting. Hence, choices A, B and C are incorrect. Choice D is the only one that is reinforcing in nature.

56. **Best answer is B.** Concept being tested is <u>Subject Verb Agreement, Pattern 3</u>. "Professionals" is the subject of the sentence. The subject is plural and hence, it needs a plural verb. The professionals make sure the issues are resolved in a timely manner.

57. **Best answer is B.** Concept being tested is <u>Adjective Phrase or Participle Phrase, Pattern 12</u>. Adjective phrases modify the subject/noun that follows the phrase. Who was citing the scientology program? Thomas was. Hence, choice B is correct.

58. **Best answer is D.** Concept being tested is <u>Subject Verb Agreement, Pattern 3</u>. "Congress" is the subject of the sentence. The subject is singular and hence, it needs a singular verb. Choice B is incorrect because congress is elected by citizens, not by a citizen. Choice D correctly matches the subject and the verb. *The Congress is instrumental in the passage of the new legislature.*

59. **Best answer is A.** Concept being tested is <u>Transitional Phrases, Pattern 1</u>. Racquetball is an indoor sport. Hence, the second sentence is contrasting the first sentence. Choices B, C and D are reinforcing in nature and hence, they are incorrect.

60. **Best answer is C.** Concept being tested is <u>Subject Pronoun Agreement, Pattern 4</u>. Nobody is singular (there is only one body, not bodies). Choices A, B and D incorrectly introduce the plural pronoun "their." Instead, choice C correctly matches the subject with the pronoun "his or her."

61. **Best answer is A.** Concept being tested is <u>Who vs Whom & Whoever vs Whomever, Pattern 5</u>. Who is used when a subject is needed. Whom is used when an object is needed. In this case, you

would answer the question with a *him/her*. I am going to prom with *her/him*. Hence, *whom* is needed.

62. ***Best answer is A.*** Concept being tested is <u>Adjective Phrase or Participle Phrase, Pattern 12</u>. Adjective phrases modify the subject/noun that follows the phrase. Who is an evangelical follower? Mary is. Only choice A places the noun/subject right next to the adjective phrase.

63. ***Best answer is B.*** Concept being tested is <u>Subject Verb Agreement, Pattern 3</u>. "Officials" is the subject of the sentence. The subject is plural and hence, it needs a plural verb. *The city officials act in the interest of the community.*

64. ***Best answer is D.*** Concept being tested is <u>Adjective Phrase or Participle Phrase, Pattern 12</u>. Adjective phrases modify the subject/noun that follows the phrase. Who is a lead singer in the band? Britney is. Hence, only choice D correctly places the noun/subject right next to the adjective phrase.

65. ***Best answer is D.*** Concept being tested is <u>Parallel Structure, Pattern 13</u>. Volcanoes erupt and form mountains.

66. ***Best answer is A.*** Concept being tested is <u>Subject Verb Agreement, Pattern 3</u>. "Chains" is the subject of the sentence. The subject is plural and hence, it needs a plural verb. The mountain chains are the result of tectonic plate movement. "Without exception" is correct.

67. ***Best answer is C.*** Concept being tested is <u>Two Commas or Two Dashes or Two Parentheses, Pattern 10</u>. Two dashes introduce parenthetical information. Remove "fastest man on earth" and read the sentence as "As expected, Bolt won the gold medal." Hence, using two dashes as in choice C is appropriate.

68. ***Best answer is B.*** Concept being tested is <u>Who vs Whom & Whoever vs Whomever, Pattern 5</u>. Whoever is used when a subject is needed. Whomever is used when an object is needed. In this case, you would answer the question with a *him/her*. Give the invitation to him/her. Hence, *whomever* is needed.

69. ***Best answer is B.*** Concept being tested is <u>Redundancy or Wordiness, Pattern 2</u>. "Imminent," "happen in the near future" and "happen soon" mean the same and hence, they are redundant. Choice B eliminates the redundancy.

70. ***Best answer is C.*** Concept being tested is <u>Redundancy or Wordiness, Pattern 2</u>. "Inadvertently" "unintentionally" and "accidently" mean the same. Choice C eliminates the redundancy.

71. ***Best answer is C.*** Concept being tested is <u>Adjective Phrase or Participle Phrase, Pattern 12</u>. Adjective phrases modify the subject/noun that follows the phrase. Who was asked about the divorce with Brad? Angelina was. Hence, choice C is the only correct answer.

72. ***Best answer is C.*** Concept being tested is <u>Exceptions of Possessive Case, Pattern 8</u>. Choice A is not proper English. Choice B does not even indicate a possessive case. For nouns ending in s, no "s" is needed after the apostrophe. Choice C is the correct possessive form involving a noun ending in s.

73. ***Best answer is A.*** Concept being tested is <u>Two Commas or Two Dashes or Two Parentheses, Pattern 10</u>. Two dashes introduce parenthetical information. Remove "tardiest employee of all" and read the sentence as "To everyone's dismay, John showed up on time." Hence, using two dashes as in choice C is appropriate.

74. ***Best answer is A.*** Concept being tested is <u>Transitional Phrases, Pattern 1</u>. The two sentences are contrasting in nature, not reinforcing. Hence, choices B, C and D are incorrect. Choice A is the only one that is showing a contrast.

75. ***Best answer is D.*** Concept being tested is <u>Two Commas or Two Dashes or Two Parentheses, Pattern 10</u>. Two dashes introduce parenthetical information. Remove "my son's chess coach" and read the sentence as "I met Mr. Smith at the tournament." Hence, using two dashes as in choice D is appropriate.

76. ***Best answer is A.*** Concept being tested is <u>Punctuation, Pattern 6</u>. Note that in choices B and C, "winning the game" is not an independent clause. Hence, a period and a semicolon are not appropriate. Choice D is using a comma to separate two independent clauses. Choice A is correct. The sentence before a colon is an independent clause. Colon is introducing a list. In this instance, the list has only one item, i.e. "winning the game."

77. ***Best answer is B.*** Concept being tested is <u>Who vs Whom & Whoever vs Whomever, Pattern 5</u>. Who is used when a subject is needed. Whom is used when an object is needed. In this case, you would answer the question with a *him/her*. I am inviting him/her to the graduation party. Hence, *whom* is needed.

78. ***Best answer is A.*** Concept being tested is <u>Adjective Phrase or Participle Phrase, Pattern 12</u>. Adjective phrases modify the subject/noun that follows the phrase. Who was known for his bold roles? Anthony was. Hence, choice A is the only correct answer.

79. ***Best answer is A.*** Concept being tested is <u>Subject Verb Agreement, Pattern 3</u>. "Archipelago" is the subject of the sentence. The subject is singular and hence, it needs a singular verb. The archipelago lies off the coast of Florida.

80. ***Best answer is C.*** Concept being tested is the <u>Exceptions of Possessive Case, Pattern 8</u>. It's means "It is." Hence, choice A is incorrect. Choice B is not a proper English phrase. Choice D introduces a plural, "their." Baby Elephant is singular. Hence, "its" is appropriate. No apostrophe needed.

81. ***Best answer is D.*** Concept being tested is <u>Redundancy or Wordiness, Pattern 2</u>. "New" means improved. Choice D eliminates redundancy.

82. ***Best answer is B.*** Concept being tested is <u>Exceptions of Possessive Case, Pattern 8</u>. Choices A and D are not proper English. For nouns ending in s, no "s" is needed after the apostrophe. Choice C incorrectly matches the beaches with "its." Instead, one should say beaches are known for *their* beauty.

83. ***Best answer is B.*** Concept being tested is <u>Two Commas or Two Dashes or Two Parentheses, Pattern 10</u>. Two dashes introduce parenthetical information. Remove "Joe Williams" and read the

sentence as "Please call my doctor tomorrow." Hence, using two dashes as in choice B is appropriate.

84. **_Best answer is B._** Concept being tested is <u>Redundancy or Wordiness, Pattern 2</u>. Choice B is concise.

85. **_Best answer is B._** Concept being tested is <u>Adjective Phrase or Participle Phrase, Pattern 12</u>. Adjective phrases modify the subject/noun that follows the phrase. Who was co-starring along-side Tommy? Harrison was. Hence, choice B is the only correct answer.

86. **_Best answer is B._** Concept being tested is <u>Who vs Whom & Whoever vs Whomever, Pattern 5</u>. Who is used when a subject is needed. Whom is used when an object is needed. In this case, you would answer the question with a _him/her_. Mary asked me to contact him/her. Hence, _whom_ is needed.

87. **_Best answer is D._** Concept being tested is <u>Transitional Phrases, Pattern 1</u>. The two sentences are reinforcing in nature, not contrasting. Hence, choices A, B and C are incorrect. Choice D is the only one that is showing a confirmation.

88. **_Best answer is B._** Concept being tested is <u>Exceptions of Possessive Case, Pattern 8</u>. Choices A and D are not proper English. For nouns ending in s, no "s" is needed after the apostrophe. Choice C does not have an apostrophe. Choice B is correct. It has an apostrophe but no "s" after the apostrophe.

89. **_Best answer is C._** Concept being tested is <u>Adjective Phrase or Participle Phrase, Pattern 12</u>. Adjective phrases modify the subject/noun that follows the phrase. Who was nominated for her role? Nicole was. Hence, choice C is the only correct answer.

90. **_Best answer is C._** Concept being tested is <u>Exceptions of Possessive Case, Pattern 8.</u> Choices A is not proper English. For nouns ending in s, no "s" is needed after the apostrophe. Choice D does not have an apostrophe. Choice B is incorrect because it says "profit are." Instead, it should say "profits are" as in choice C.

91. **_Best answer is D._** Concept being tested is <u>Transitional Phrases, Pattern 1</u>. The two sentences are reinforcing in nature. Hence, choices A, B and C are incorrect. Although choices C and D could work, choice D is better because it is adding on to what students are expected to do.

92. **_Best answer is B._** Concept being tested is <u>Who vs Whom & Whoever vs Whomever, Pattern 5</u>. Who is used when a subject is needed. Whom is used when an object is needed. In this case, you would answer the question with a _him/her_. I trust him/her. Hence, _whom_ is needed.

93. **_Best answer is B._** Concept being tested is <u>Transitional Phrases, Pattern 1</u>. The two sentences are contrasting in nature. Hence, choices A, C and D are incorrect. Choice B correctly introduces the contrast.

94. **_Best answer is B._** Concept being tested is <u>Two Commas or Two Dashes or Two Parentheses, Pattern 10</u>. In this case, choice B is an illustration of correct usage of two dashes.

95. **Best answer is B**. Concept being tested is the <u>Exceptions of Possessive Case, Pattern 8</u>. It's means "It is." Hence, choice A is incorrect. Choice C is not a proper English phrase. Choice D introduces a plural, "their." Team is singular. Hence, "its" is appropriate. No apostrophe is needed.

96. **Best answer is B.** Concept being tested is <u>Redundancy or Wordiness, Pattern 2</u>. Choice B eliminates redundancy.

97. **Best answer is A.** Concept being tested is <u>Transitional Phrases, Pattern 1</u>. Sentence is enumerating examples of national parks. Choices B, C and D do not fit well with the transition.

98. **Best answer is C.** Concept being tested is <u>Redundancy or Wordiness, Pattern 2</u>. New and innovation mean the same. Hence, eliminate choices A, B and D.

99. **Best answer is A.** Concept being tested is <u>Transitional Phrases, Pattern 1</u>. You need a contrast. Choices B, C and D are reinforcing in nature and hence, they are not the right transitions.

100. **Best answer is D.** Concept being tested is <u>Redundancy or Wordiness, Pattern 2</u>. Past and history mean the same. Hence, eliminate choices A, B and C.

101. **Best answer is D.** Concept being tested is <u>Transitional Phrases, Pattern 1</u>. Chess and mountain climbing both need patience. Hence, choices A, B, and C are incorrect.

102. **Best answer is B.** Concept being tested is <u>Redundancy or Wordiness, Pattern 2</u>. Reverted and back mean the same. Hence, eliminate choices A, C and D.

103. **Best answer is D.** Concept being tested is <u>Transitional Phrases, Pattern 1</u>. The meeting was cancelled because the chair person was ill. Choice D correctly introduces the transition.

104. **Best answer is D.** Concept being tested is <u>Transitional Phrases, Pattern 1</u>. John is not able to pay his bills because he lost his job. Hence, choices A, B and C are incorrect. Choice D correctly introduces the transition.

105. **Best answer is D.** Concept being tested is <u>Redundancy or Wordiness, Pattern 2</u>. At first and initially mean the same. Hence, eliminate choices A, B and C.

106. **Best answer is D.** Concept being tested is <u>Redundancy or Wordiness, Pattern 2</u>. Rained for ten days means it rained consecutively. The phrase "consecutively" is redundant. Choice D eliminates the redundancy.

107. **Best answer is A.** Concept being tested is <u>Two Commas or Two Dashes or Two Parentheses, Pattern 10</u>. In this case, choice A is an illustration of correct usage of two dashes.

108. **Best answer is C**. Concept being tested is the <u>Exceptions of Possessive Case, Pattern 8.</u> It's means "It is." Hence, choice B is incorrect. Choice A is not a proper English phrase. Choice D introduces a plural, "their." The city is singular and hence, "its" is appropriate. No Apostrophe is needed.